PROCESS IMPROVEMENT
Enhancing Your Organization's Effectiveness

Eileen Flanigan
Jon Scott

A FIFTY-MINUTE™ SERIES BOOK

DISTRIBUTED BY

FLEX TRAINING LTD NC.
9-15 Hitchin Street
Baldock
Herts. SG7 6AL
Tel: 01462 895544
Fax: 01462 892417

PROCESS IMPROVEMENT
Enhancing Your Organization's Effectiveness

Eileen Flanigan
Jon Scott

CREDITS
Managing Editor: **Kathleen Barcos**
Editor: **Christopher Carrigan**
Typesetting: **ExecuStaff**
Artwork: **Ralph Mapson**
Cover Design: **Carol Harris**

Copyright © 1995 by Crisp Publications, Inc.

Printed in the United States of America by Bawden Printing Company.

Distribution to the U.S. Trade:

National Book Network, Inc.
4720 Boston Way
Lanham, MD 20706
1-800-462-6420

Library of Congress Catalog Card Number 95-67042
Flanigan, Eileen and Jon Scott
Process Improvement
ISBN 1-56052-322-0

This book is printed
on recyclable paper
with soy ink.

ABOUT THE BOOK

Process Improvement is not like most books. It has a unique self-paced format that encourages the reader to become involved in the exercises, activities and assessments that are found throughout its pages.

The objective of this book is to provide a resource that will help people build their skills to become more effective at increasing customer value through process improvement.

Process Improvement can be used effectively in a number of ways. Here are some possibilities:

► **Individual Study.** Because the book is self-instructional, all that is needed is a quiet place, some time and a pencil. Completing the activities and exercises will provide you a map to the rewards of process improvement.

► **Workshops and Seminars.** The book is ideal for preassigned reading prior to a workshop or seminar. With the basics in hand, the quality of participation should improve. This book is also extremely effective when distributed at the beginning of a session and used as the course workbook.

► **Remote Location Training.** Copies can be sent to those not able to attend "home office" training sessions.

► **Informal Study Groups.** Thanks to the format, brevity and low cost, this book is ideal for "brown bag" or other informal group sessions. Gather your team, department members or peers together and spend some time preparing for an exciting future.

There are other possibilities that will surface as you go through this book, so grab a pencil and get started. Enjoy!

ABOUT THE AUTHORS

Eileen Flanigan, MBA, is a widely experienced consultant, meeting facilitator, and corporate trainer specializing in team dynamics, facilitation, customer service and process change.

Eileen began her focus on process improvement while visiting companies throughout Southeast Asia that had relocated operations from the United States. This highlighted the need to re-examine the current structure and practices of leadership, communication and process change within the business community.

The exploration has led to a career focus on facilitation, change and improving communication with companies as diverse as Volkswagen USA, Novell, and Hughes Aircraft Company.

Jon Scott, MBA, MS in Systems Management, has extensive experience in business, technology, and education specializing in corporate change, process improvement, team building, facilitation and customer service skills.

Since the early 1980s, Jon has focused primarily on becoming a change agent specializing in the rapid functional improvement of operations deemed critical by company leadership. These real world, hands-on experiences have developed and honed his direct, practical approach to unleashing people's potential in the workplace.

CONTENTS

INTRODUCTION

Striving to deliver the best value to the customer is mandatory for survival in today's marketplace. This is true regardless of whether you are the company president or work in the mail room. We all have customers, internal and external. We all have pressures to contribute to the success of our organizations. We all want to contribute, but where do we begin? We hear so much about reengineering and process improvement, but what is it and how do we actually use it?

In workplaces across the world, people are struggling to know how and where to begin in their efforts to change and improve. They do not want more theory. They do not want to spend millions of dollars on consultants. They want practical, easy-to-understand instructions.

This book is aimed at the reader who wants to personally understand and apply process improvement techniques, either as a doer or a leader.

This book is for the reader that wants to:

- Quickly grasp what process improvement is all about

- Learn enough about specific tools and techniques to be able to apply this to their own individual situation

This book is geared for the person who is looking for a practical guide to process improvement.

It is a fast-changing world. Those that do not keep up will be left behind. This book allows the reader to quickly grasp process improvement tools and techniques and apply them in their own area. The application of these process improvement tools will demonstrate a capacity for not only embracing change but also for leading the change process. This will provide opportunities for recognition, enhanced job security and increase the potential for promotion.

In this time of company downsizing, the person who grasps the opportunity to bring value to their organization through the application of process improvement tools and techniques is the person most likely to be retained.

P A R T

I

What Is Process Improvement?

THE CONCEPT IS SIMPLE!

Process improvement is a way to look at the world that allows you to do things better, cheaper or faster. By using the ideas behind process improvement, you can create products or services that are vastly superior to your competition. This advantage allows you to create a large and loyal group of customers that will last at least until someone else comes up with a better product than yours. Because there are always competitors who are looking for ways to improve their products and increase their share of the customers, you must keep looking for ways to improve your products.

There are two major "process-oriented" approaches to consider using to keep improving your products or services: one is generally referred to as *process improvement* and the other is generally referred to as *process reengineering*. Although the end goal of both approaches is to do things better, faster and cheaper, there are some differences in how each approach begins.

Process reengineering begins by assuming that everything currently being done is suspect and you should start with a blank sheet of paper. Process reengineering typically aims for:

- Widespread, radical change

- Improvements of 100 percent or more

- Revolution not evolution to current ways of doing business

An example of a process reengineering project is: The company decides to combine the sales and order processing departments and create a totally new way of generating and accepting customer orders.

Process improvement is typically thought of as an approach that aims for:

- Incremental change

- Improvements of 25 percent or more

- Evolution to current way of doing business

An example of a process improvement project is: The company decides to streamline the order entry process.

THE CONCEPT IS SIMPLE! (continued)

Why Not Always Use Process Reengineering if the Payoff Is Higher?

Because of these differences in the amount of "payoff" or improvement promised between reengineering and process improvement, it is usual to find that high-level people within the company want reengineering projects to be implemented. The high-level people want large amounts of improvements, which is OK, but because they are so far removed from the day-to-day detail, they normally drastically underestimate what it will take to successfully complete a reengineering project.

Key Idea: The larger the project scope, the larger the potential payoff *and* risk.

The high-level people know that they need to do something and they feel the need to do it now. Normally this leads to a large amount of people being involved in a process reengineering project without a clear idea of how to proceed. Or sometimes this leads to a process reengineering project being half-implemented and then getting stuck.

Fortunately, you can avoid a considerable amount of the usual process reengineering pitfalls by combining the best of the process reengineering approach with the best of the process improvement approach. They actually have quite a bit in common. Both reengineering and process improvement:

- ✔ Use the customer as the starting point

- ✔ Require participation

- ✔ Take a process view

- ✔ Depend upon measurements

- ✔ Require some training and preparation

- ✔ Drive positive change to help create a better product or service

- ✔ Work as well in a service business as in manufacturing

From this perspective, process reengineering and process improvement have quite a bit in common. The approach of this book is that any process project that you start should:

- Question whether the process is even needed (process reengineering idea)

- Throw out the process if it is not needed (process reengineering idea)

- Improve the process if the process is needed (process improvement idea)

You decide if you want to call this approach process reengineering or process improvement.

Key Idea: Stay focused on the end goal. Don't get caught up in the jargon!

For the remainder of this book, you will see the term process improvement used to describe the combined approaches. These methods recommended give you the best chance possible to do things better, faster and cheaper and create a large and loyal group of customers.

Process versus Task

Process improvement depends upon a process view of the world. This process view is different from a traditional task view.

Most management efforts, since the industrial revolution, focused on breaking work down into small steps. One person would be assigned to each step. These small steps were the basis for the assembly line. The assembly line concept worked well for many years and continues to work best when the goal is to turn out a large number of things that are exactly the same. Unfortunately for the traditional assembly line producers, some companies figured out how to provide customers with products that offered greater choices, shorter delivery times, and higher quality—all at a cheaper price. One of the major ways they did this was to look at the work flow from a process view.

6

THE CONCEPT IS SIMPLE! (continued)

A process view is defined as the sequence of things done to produce an output. A task is just one individual step in the process.

INPUT → Task A + Task B + Task C + Task D = OUTPUT

▶ An input is whatever you need to start the process.

▶ The tasks are the individual things you add to the input.

▶ The output is the thing you give your customer.

PROCESS	TASKS
Make a cake	Pick a recipe, get ingredients, pre-heat oven, mix ingredients, bake in oven, cool the layers, assemble the layers, mix frosting, frost the cake

In most cases, a business process will involve multiple people and multiple departments. If we focus on the process, we can see everything it takes to deliver the output. This allows us to optimize the entire process instead of the output of just one person or just one area or just one task.

Key Idea: Focus first on WHAT needs to be done to satisfy the customer, not who is doing it.

A process view looks at a collection of tasks to determine:

• How could we better group the tasks together?

• Does each task add value to the output?

• What does the customer need and want as the output of this process?

• How could we either reduce the time of the tasks or eliminate them?

The process view is the cornerstone for applying Process Improvement techniques.

HOW PROCESS IMPROVEMENT FITS IN WITH OTHER WAYS TO IMPROVE

If you went to your local bookstore, you could find quite a few books that all address how to make your company more competitive. Those books would cover topics like:

- Success through Empowerment

- Success through Teams

- Success through Self-Managed Teams

- Success through Quality Teams

  - Success according to Deming

  - Success according to Juran

  - Success according to "insert the name of most Fortune 500 CEOs"

  - Success according to the Japanese

    - Success through Flattening the Organization

    - Success through Outsourcing

    - Success through Rightsizing

All of these concepts emphasize a different aspect of what it takes to be successful in today's world. Some are more applicable at certain times than others. Some are more specific in their prescription than others. Some are more philosophical. Some are very difficult to implement if you aren't the CEO.

HOW PROCESS IMPROVEMENT FITS IN WITH OTHER WAYS TO IMPROVE (continued)

Process improvement borrows freely from the best of the above. But unlike a majority of these techniques, process improvement ideas can be applied at any level of the business and can start right with you. If you have any desire to improve, then you can apply and follow the three rules of process improvement!

The Three Rules of Process Improvement

Rule #1: FOCUS on your CUSTOMER.

Rule #2: Use the PROCESS VIEW to deliver what the CUSTOMER WANTS.

Rule #3: When you think you're done, BEGIN THE CYCLE AGAIN.

These rules can be quite different from what you or your company is used to doing. The table that follows can be used as an indicator of where you and your company are right now. Check one statement from each row that most fits you and where you work.

COMPLETE THE FOLLOWING SURVEY FOR A PROCESS IMPROVEMENT QUICK-CHECK

Survey: "Where Am I?"

	A	B
1.	☐ I know who my customer is.	☐ I am not sure who my customer is.
2.	☐ I talk directly to my customer and ask for feedback on what they want.	☐ I give my customer what I know they need.
3.	☐ I am measured by how well I satisfy my customer.	☐ I am measured on how well my supervisor likes me.
4.	☐ The way to get ahead is to be innovative and work for changes.	☐ The way to get ahead is to do my job.
5.	☐ I understand the department and company vision.	☐ I do the work that is put in front of me.
6.	☐ I am part of a team.	☐ I focus on my task.
7.	☐ My ideas are acted upon.	☐ My ideas are lost in the shuffle.
8.	☐ My boss will get ahead by satisfying the customer.	☐ My boss will get ahead by having more people in the department.
9.	☐ I spend a large amount of my time thinking of ways to improve things.	☐ I spend most of my time doing my job and protecting myself.
10.	☐ Learning new things is encouraged.	☐ Training is not encouraged.
11.	☐ I can make a difference.	☐ It is up to someone else to make a difference.
	_____ "A" TOTAL	_____ "B" TOTAL

Add the number of items you checked in the "A" column and then the "B" column. The higher the "A" score, the more you are already using process improvement ideas. The higher the "B" score, the more opportunity you have for improvement.

HOW PROCESS IMPROVEMENT FITS IN WITH OTHER WAYS TO IMPROVE (continued)

What Value Does Process Improvement Offer?

There are many individual and organizational benefits to making process improvement part of your workplace.

> **Key Idea:** Increasing customer value and doing things better, cheaper, faster must be part of the job, not a separate "buzzword."

The following list includes benefits mentioned most by people who have participated in making process improvement part of their way of doing business.

Place a ✔ by those that you think that you would like as part of your life.

- ☐ Feeling of contribution and accomplishment

- ☐ Feeling of pride in your work

- ☐ Increasing job security

- ☐ Enjoying work more

- ☐ Working hard, but having fun too

- ☐ Creating satisfied customers

- ☐ Increasing promotion and earning potential

- ☐ Feeling of focus and forward movement

In addition to these personal benefits, the company benefits too. Greater customer satisfaction leads to more customers. More customers create more sales and more profits. More sales and profits create company growth. Growth creates more opportunities for all.

Ensuring Successful Process Improvement

There are some major benefits to be gained by making process improvement a part of your life in the workplace. There are also some specific actions that you must be willing to take if you expect to gain the benefits. You must:

- Take risks

- Be enthusiastic

- Set the example

- Educate yourself

- Be part of a team

- Take the initiative

- Be part of the solution

- Be prepared for criticism

- Focus on customer and process

- Move from thinking "I" to thinking "We"

- Say what you will do and then do what you say

- Be open to change and try new and different things

- Accept individual responsibility for your own situation

- Do not blame or use excuses as a substitute for personal effort

This list is very easy to compile, but difficult to live up to on a daily basis. Competition is taking its toll on companies and individuals that do not adapt. Now is a wonderful opportunity for those who can change!

YOUR CHALLENGE IS CLEAR!

"Everybody wants to go to heaven; They just don't want to die to get there."

—Mark Twain

If this were really easy everyone would be doing it. Those that make process improvement work say that the rewards are worth the effort. Have realistic expectations for your first project. You should be prepared for a wide range of reactions from your co-workers, subordinates and supervisors. There is a pretty good chance that you will get some negative reactions. These reactions are mostly driven by fear of the unknown. You will probably hear comments like:

- "That'll never work here."

- "They tried that before."

- "You have REAL work to do."

- "Are you trying to make us look bad?"

- "As long as you do it on your own time."

- "That's nice, but there is nothing we can do."

There will be different agendas by different people. There will be different priorities. Not everyone will share the same sense of urgency. In short, *expect difficulty!* But there are ways to overcome this resistance.

Overcome the Doom Predictors!

Seek like-minded people to help you. In every group there are some "doom predictors" and some who want to make a positive difference. If you have to work, why not make it a positive experience? The effort is worth it.

Don't let yourself get sucked into the mud by the doom predictors. Stick with phrases like "Perhaps you are right, but I think I'll try this anyway" or "If it doesn't work then at least we will know" or "It can't hurt." Do not act superior. You want everyone to feel comfortable and willing to work with you.

If you keep at it, a strange thing will happen. First, some people will become curious about what you are doing. They will notice that you are enjoying your job more. They will see that you are making a positive difference. Since people really want to do a good job, they will want to get in on the act. Before long, people will wonder why they waited so long to work this way.

Work Your Problem!

It all starts with you. It doesn't matter if you are the CEO or work in the mail room. What matters is your willingness to make a personal commitment to continually improve whatever your job might be. What matters is your willingness to try new things to delight your customers.

Take a moment and review your own reactions to what you have just read in Part I.

How do you know you are ready to make a change for the better?

_____

_____

What will you have to change about yourself to make process improvement work for you?

_____

_____

Think of your own job and the people you work with. Who are the ones who will support new ways?

_____

_____

How can you get them to help you?

_____

_____

Think of past experiences that your company has had with trying new ways. What lessons have you learned from those experiences?

_____

_____

P A R T

II

Identifying the Players

THE CUSTOMER IS #1

It is hard to imagine a successful business without a satisfied customer—in fact, one of the definitions of a successful business **is** a satisfied customer! If customers are that important, then knowing what your customers want can make the difference between success and failure.

First you need to identify who your customer is. Your customer is anyone internal to your company or external to your company who comes in contact with the product or output of your work. If you play a role in supporting the person who ultimately uses the end product, then you are supporting an "external customer." If you play a part in the intermediate process and interact with people or departments within your own company, then you are supporting an "internal customer." Each of these customers is an important player in your efforts to improve and will provide valuable input if asked. Sometimes the input is offered without being requested—this comes from especially valuable customers!

 Key Idea: A customer is anyone whose satisfaction depends upon your process.

Customers can be demanding, but they can also be your best marketing. We are more likely to try a new business or purchase a product if someone we know has had a positive experience with the service or product. This kind of word-of-mouth doesn't spend a penny of your advertising dollar and carries more weight than any ad you could produce.

It is also important to remember that a *dissatisfied* customer tells an average of 12 people about their unsatisfactory experience. These 12 tell another 12 and so on. It doesn't take long before the negative reports spread like wildfire. We tend to believe what we hear through our friends and co-workers. So keep in mind the challenge a company, or a department within a company, has when it's received bad publicity.

Your process output is what matters to your customer. You either have a product that your external customer values and is willing to pay money for or you go out of business. When applying the tools of process improvement, you want to lay a foundation based on what your customer values. Once you have identified your customers' values and needs, you use them to drive your improvement process. It's so much easier to hit the target when you know what you are aiming for. Allow your customers to define the target!

THE CUSTOMER IS #1 (continued)

Working with External Customers

Defining what your customer values is the first step. The equation below defines value from your customer's point of view.

$$\text{Value} = \frac{\text{Quality}}{\text{Cost}}$$

The higher the quality and the lower the cost, the more the customer perceives value. A person may gladly pay more for a product or service if they feel the quality is high enough to bring them greater value. When given a choice, customers go where they feel they get the most value.

The job in front of you is to identify how *your* customer defines value. It is important to focus on the customers' definition of value and not your own. The only way you can really know how your customer defines value is to ask!

GETTING CUSTOMER FEEDBACK

We will be discussing two different types of survey tools: customer value feedback and industry benchmarking. First, let's focus on the customer by discussing customer value feedback.

Customer value feedback is *not* a customer satisfaction survey. That type of survey measures how the customer feels your company is performing. What you want to capture in your customer value feedback is *what* is important to your customer and *how* important is each item they indicate. When gathering customer value feedback, remember:

- ► Give the opportunity for open-ended discussions of expectations and desires whenever possible.

- ► Solicit information from both existing customers and those you have identified as potential customers. Both groups will give you valuable information that can lead to improvement opportunities.

- ► Have a cross-section of people conduct the feedback sessions. You lower the possibility of bias as well as increase the buy-in of those people who will be implementing the changes.

Listed below are the various ways that you can gather information for your customer value feedback. Do not limit yourself only to your customers, sometimes the competitor's customers are goldmines of information.

METHOD	PURPOSE
One on One	Use when you have lots of time and want detailed information.
Small Group Meetings	Use to sample a larger customer group.
Observation	See how people use your product or service. Use with a small, defined customer group.
Telephone	Works well if you want to sample a large number of customers in remote locations.
Written Feedback	Requires minimal employee time and yet can gather information from a broad customer base.

First, decide the method you want to use to gather your information, then formulate your questions. Remember to keep them clear, short and open-ended to encourage feedback.

GETTING CUSTOMER FEEDBACK (continued)

Sample Questions:

► When you recall your last experience with our company/organization, what stands out the most?

► What are some of the things you would like us to keep doing?

► What are some of the things you would like us to stop doing or to change?

► Is there a new service/product that you would like us to provide?

► What is your overall impression after dealing with our company/organization?

Take the opportunity now to put together some questions to ask your customers.

Question 1: _____

_____

Question 2: _____

_____

Question 3: _____

_____

Question 4: _____

_____

Question 5: _____

_____

Key Idea: Don't assume you know what the customer thinks—Ask!

Expanding the Role of the Internal Customer

Everything we have discussed until now applies to both internal and external customers. Now we will expand on the role of the internal customer.

> ## *Pop Quiz*
>
> Your organization is responsible for the assembly of the keyboards for a major computer company. Your assembly work is done early in the manufacturing process and you rarely see the entire finished product that goes out the door to the customer.
>
> Since you never see the person who buys the computer, who is your customer? _____

If you work on part of a product, process some of the documents, or handle a behind-the-scenes job, you still have very important customers that you service. It can be easy to forget when you don't deal with the end purchaser, that there are products/services that you "sell," processes that you use, and certainly customers that you support!

Virtually every company has internal operations that are critical to its overall success. The internal customer value survey will help you discover what is required to meet the needs of those people who receive your outputs as you all work to satisfy the ultimate customer.

A good place to begin is with the customer value feedback discussed earlier. Develop your survey and approach those people or departments that are on the receiving end of your outputs. Treating your internal people as both customers and teammates can be a real competitive advantage. Frequently it is internal difficulties that lead to the inability to properly respond to the external customer. These internal difficulties can lead to competitive, adversarial relationships between the very organizations that need to cooperate toward servicing the customer. View the operations or functions that follow your functions *as your customer*. When treated as such, you all remain focused on your ultimate goal—satisfied customers, profitability, growth and employment!

THE NEXT MOST IMPORTANT PERSON

You have read about the external customer and the internal customer. Now let's talk about the next most important person in process improvement: You.

This may come as a surprise to you, but regardless of where you are in the company or your department, you have the ability to change things. Even if you are not the formal leader, you can set the example for all. Even if you are not the president of the company, you can work to make your customers delighted with your process output. You may feel powerless, but there is power in working to better satisfy your customer and to improve your processes.

If you are the company president, then it is easier to get process improvement projects started all across your company. But what happens if your employees don't participate? You have big trouble! As an employee, at any level of a company, you are an individual person who makes decisions on a daily basis. You decide how much to give to your job. You decide how much to risk! You decide whether you are just putting in your time or whether you are proud of what you do! Your decisions can mark you as leader and contributor or just another body taking up space. It is your choice.

Of course, you can be a "fence-sitter," like most people are, and never decide.

Key Idea: If you do want to make a difference then the best place to begin is with yourself.

You can be a leader/contributor by acting as a leader/contributor. Being a leader/contributor does not mean that you ignore direction given to you by your supervisor. Being a leader does mean that you can help lead, contribute, and support changes necessary to improve.

Being a leader/contributor is not an easy task. It is not easy to speak out against the opinion of your peers. A leader/contributor can be a very lonely person. It is easier to be just another body taking up space. This is true until either the company goes out of business or the company lay-offs begin.

The following are some differences between leaders/contributors and bodies taking up space:

Leaders/Contributors Are More Concerned About:	Bodies Taking Up Space Are More Concerned About:
Doing what is right	Doing what is required
Vision for the future	What we did a year ago
Giving	Getting
Customers	Themselves
Accepting responsibility	Avoiding responsibility
Encouraging change	Fighting all change
Caring	Apathy
Process	Fire fighting
Is it my best?	Is it good enough?
How can I improve?	It was good enough before
Attitude of ownership	Just a hired hand
Love it, change it or leave	Stay and complain

Whatever your current level in your company, you may wish to ask yourself if you are currently acting as a leader/contributor or a body taking up space or a fence-sitter. There are still way too many managers that qualify as a body taking up space or a fence-sitter. Do not use them to make excuses for your situation. Your efforts as a leader/contributor are the engines that drive process improvement and increase customer value. You offer unique capabilities, if you decide to get off the fence and into the game.

THE NEXT MOST IMPORTANT PERSON
(continued)

If you are already acting as a leader/contributor, then you are one who has perfected the ability to allow yourself and others to maximize their contributions. You may be in a management position, a member of a successful team, sponsoring teams that reach their goals or simply a valued member of an organization where change is embraced as an opportunity.

> **Key Idea:** Leadership is not a formal position, it is earned through actions.

Questions on Leadership

Who have you known in the past that you would identify as a true leader?

_____

_____

What specific skills did they use to bring out the best in others?

_____

_____

Which of these skills are you most comfortable using?

_____

_____

Are you ready to assume a leader/contributor role in your organization?

_____

_____

Work Your Problem!

The time has arrived to identify your customers' values. Process improvement itself is a step-by-step process and your customers are where you begin.

Who are your key customers? _____

_____

Are they external or internal? _____

_____

What products or services do you currently provide? _____

_____

How can you best determine your customer's expectations? _____

_____

Do your products or services consistently meet or exceed customer expectations?

_____

_____

What tells you if your products or services are improving? _____

_____

How will you describe to your customers what you are up to? _____

_____

When will you get started? _____

_____

PART

III

Ensuring Success

FIND PROCESSES THAT NEED IMPROVEMENT

If you want to grill a hamburger, then don't buy fish at the supermarket. The same is true with your first process improvement projects. What you start with will have a large impact on what you end with. Your first project is important because it will set the expectations for those that follow. It is OK to stack the deck in your favor! Here are some clear guidelines to follow that will increase the chance of your success.

For your first project, pick a project where:

- Most people agree that the problem is one that needs to be solved

- The problem is tied to a process not a single individual

- The process has a definable, accessible customer

- The process fits in with your current responsibilities

- Goals can be attained in 9 to 12 weeks

- Goals and results can be objectively measured

This first project can be a pilot project. You are going to learn from it. Do not try and change the world this first time. After you practice a little then you can go after the "big one."

 Key Idea: Define the scope of your project and stick to it!

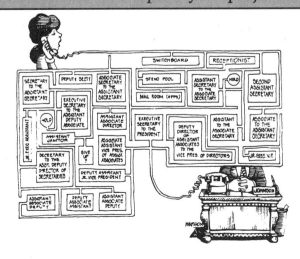

FIND PROCESSES THAT NEED IMPROVEMENT (continued)

If you are still stuck at what to select for your first project, here are some more clues. Look for:

- ✔ Piles of paper

- ✔ Piles of anything sitting around

- ✔ Problem is standing joke in the company

- ✔ Major source of customer complaints

- ✔ A "black hole"

- ✔ Multiple hand-offs to get the whole job done

- ✔ Errors or scrapping continue to occur

- ✔ Plentiful procedures and mountains of manuals

- ✔ High employee turnover

- ✔ Low morale

- ✔ The process takes too long. . .

- ✔ The process costs to much. . .

- ✔ There are no current measurements in place for success or tracking procedures

- ✔ Expedite tags are used

- ✔ Inspectors are inspecting

- ✔ Counters are counting

- ✔ Approvers are approving

Well, you get the idea. . . .

List three processes within your area of expertise that are ripe for improvement:

1. _____

2. _____

3. _____

Now that you have narrowed down the field, you need to start keeping track of how the processes are performing in an objective and quantifiable manner.

Measurements and Benchmarking

Measurements and benchmarking are two critical tools in process improvement. Normally, this is where you get a lecture on SPC charts and linear regression. Instead, let's put the two tools of measurement and benchmarking in perspective.

Measurements at Work and Play

If you like to play any games at all, then you know how to keep score. We learned that as little kids. We did it as kids because it was fun! If you jumped rope then you counted to see how many times you could go without missing! If you climbed trees, you tried to climb the tallest one. Benchmarking was knowing how much faster than you your brother could run and was he getting faster or slower.

As adults, we still keep and compare scores. It still is fun in some areas of our lives. It is fun to watch a TV game show. They keep score. It is fun to watch a football game. How much fun would it be if they didn't keep score? *Not much!*

For some reason, just by keeping score, people want to improve against that score. You do not hear people say, "Gosh, I know I could do worse if I really tried!" People want to do better, not worse. But how do they know, if there are no measures?

FIND PROCESSES THAT NEED IMPROVEMENT (continued)

So why, if measuring is so much fun, don't we do more of it in the workplace? There are really several reasons why more companies, managers and individuals do not use measurements in the workplace. The four major reasons for avoiding measurements in the workplace are:

REASON #1: *Employees fear and mistrust measurements.*

REASON #2: *There is a general lack of understanding of what or how to measure.*

REASON #3: *The results of measurements are typically not shared in an open manner.*

REASON #4: *Most people make the process of measuring harder than it needs to be.*

Let's explore each of these areas in more detail.

REASON #1: *Employees fear and mistrust measurements.*

It is true. People are afraid and wary of being measured in the workplace. It brings to mind management standing over them with stopwatches. Any hint of you being the "Mad Malicious Measuring Monster" will kill your project before it can even see the light of day.

> **Key Idea:** Measurements must be used to measure and improve the process, not punish people. By keeping measurements, we can tell whether the process is improving.

REASON #2: *There is a general lack of understanding of what or how to measure.*

Measurements, for your first projects, should focus on:

- How long it takes from beginning to end within the process?

- How many items go through the process per hour, day, week, etc.?

- How many of the items are 100 percent correct?

- How many items are waiting to begin the process?

- How long have these items been waiting?

Do not focus on cost savings for your first project. You want to avoid a cost-savings focus for several reasons:

1. Cost reductions, by themselves, are usually a demotivator to people

2. Cost savings are associated with people losing their jobs

3. Cost savings are putting money in other people's pockets, not mine

Key Idea: Cost savings can be had by focusing on cycle time, quality and responsiveness. You get the benefit anyway!

FIND PROCESSES THAT NEED IMPROVEMENT (continued)

REASON #3: *The results of measurements are typically not shared in an open manner.*

For some reason, we think that we have to keep measurements secret. Remember, we are measuring a process, not a person. All results should be posted in areas where everyone can see them. Easy-to-understand graphs are best.

Everyone affected should be encouraged to participate. Anyone involved in a process that is being measured should be given a chance to help develop the measurements. They should also see the results as soon as they are available. In a process improvement project, secrets are not your friend.

REASON #4: *Most people make the process of measuring harder than it needs to be.*

Keep It Simple

There is an old story about a consultant who was called into a steel mill to improve productivity. The mill was operating at three-shift capacity. All the consultant did was to count the number of steel pours done on the first shift. He took a piece of chalk and scrawled the following on the concrete floor outside the break room:

"1st shift: 20 pours"

Now what do you think the second and third shift did? In the space of a week, the productivity had drastically increased.

Did they have to buy a computer system to implement their measurement system? Keep it simple. Make it understandable. Let the people doing the process be the ones keeping score.

Measure the Pulse Points

There is virtually an unlimited number of medical diagnostic tests that can be run on the human body. Thank goodness we don't get them all every time we go to the doctor's office. Fortunately, there are a few vital signs that can indicate our general health. The same is true for your business process. Here are a few more helpful hints to make sure your measurement program measures up!

- Measure what is important to your customer

- Measure logical outcomes of your process

- Measure what you would like to see improved

- Measure things using common terminology

HOW GOOD IS GOOD?

So now you have some wonderful charts. So what! Now you need to set some goals for improvement and track your progress against those goals.

There are several ways to set improvement goals. One way is to ask your customers what they expect from you and to use that as a goal. Another way is to pick an arbitrary goal like "25 percent improvement." You can also try and find out what your competition is doing and use that as a performance goal.

If you expect to achieve your goal, however it was set, then the goal must be specific, measurable and easily understandable to all the people involved. Some examples of goals might be:

► Shorten the cycle time from receipt of a customer order to order delivery of 10 days to 2 days. Do this within 8 weeks.

► Identify and eliminate 50 percent of the non-value added steps in the travel expense report process within 12 weeks of project start.

Don't Forget Benchmarking

Benchmarking goes hand in hand with measurements, setting goals, and customer value. Benchmarking is trying to find out how far, how fast and in which direction other companies are moving. You get their scores and then compare yours against theirs. Then, you estimate how much they are going to improve in the future if they keep their current pace. This tells you what your goals must be if you want to stay in the race.

There are two critical parts to successful benchmarking. They are:

► Getting access to meaningful, current industry data

► Making sure when you compare yours to theirs that it is apples to apples

There are several ways to go about getting benchmarking data, including the following.

- Check out your industry or trade associations

- Look for a non-competitor who collects similar data

- Create an industry study using a local college

- Use your library to research the process

- Talk to your suppliers

- Talk with customers who use your competitors

If you get hung up trying to get benchmarking data, do not let that stop your project. Although it is important to know where you stand against your competition, that should not stop you from measuring and challenging yourself to improve your processes.

Knowing What to Expect Really Helps!

Usually, there are some common reactions at this point. If this is your first project, you may feel overwhelmed. That is understandable. After all, this is all new. Remember that at least you are trying to make a difference. If you plan for your success and then just take it one step at a time, you will do fine.

PLAN FOR YOUR SUCCESS

Planning is critically important to the success of your first process improvement project. Planning is another way of saying that we have given some thought to what we want to do before we do it.

There are two parts to successfully planning your project: narrowing the field and assembling the project plan. First, you need to narrow down the field to pick the process to tackle that is most likely to ensure your success. Some projects are doomed before they even get launched. By using the ideas presented here, you should be able to avoid that.

After you have selected the right process to improve, the second step is putting together your project plan. A project plan lets you accomplish the most in the shortest period of time. Think of it as the map that you will use to guide you to your end goal. Without the map, you might find your destination, but it would probably take longer. The last section of this part will help you develop your map.

Pick the Right Process

For your first project, selecting the right process to begin with is key. Earlier on in this section you identified processes that are ripe for improvement. Now let's screen them to pick the one most likely to succeed. The easiest way to do this is to use the following checklist.

Criteria for Picking the Right Process

For each of your processes identified as ripe for improvement, complete the following checklist:

☐ Obviously linked to business/department goals

☐ Process is highly visible

☐ Perception exists that process is "broken"

☐ Change can be accomplished in short time frame (3–6 months)

☐ Achievement of process improvement is likely (keep it simple)

☐ Improvements are visible and measurable

☐ Scope of the process is within your control

☐ Other organizations involved are interested in participating

☐ Minimum dollars required

☐ There is strong interest in tackling this process

The more items you checked for any one process, the greater your chance of success.

Key Idea: All things being equal, pick the process that generates the strongest interest.

One last word before you select your process for improvement. There are some mistakes that are commonly made at this point of process selection. Take a minute to review these before making a final decision on selecting your process for improvement.

PLAN FOR YOUR SUCCESS (continued)

Common Mistakes in Process Selection

1. **Focusing on cost savings as the main reason for process selection!**

   Too much focus on cost savings as the main reason for selecting a process for improvement will likely cause the employees to think their jobs are in jeopardy. If they think that, it is unlikely that they will be supportive.

   Focus instead on increased customer value, cycle time reductions, flexibility and quality improvements. If you focus on these items, you are very likely to get cost savings anyway.

2. **Picking a process already in transition (trying to hit a moving target)!**

   If a process is highly visible and it is thought to be broken, there may be someone or some team already trying to change it. Make sure that the process you select is not in the middle of a change.

   Reasons to avoid processes in transition include (a) It is a more complex task to make changes when you do not have a stable baseline, (b) It is difficult to measure the improvements.

   Focus instead on an established process that has been working that way for awhile.

3. **Underestimating the effort required!**

   Estimating is the process of looking into the future and gauging what it will take to do something. Most people, especially if they know a little about the subject, have a tendency to underestimate the time or resources required to improve a process and make that change stick.

   Focus on picking a small process for your first project. If you have access to people who have done this before, use them as a resource. As you gain experience, then you will be better equipped to tackle the tougher processes. This is definitely an area where it is better to walk before you run.

Now that you have come this far you should be able to select the process that you would like to improve with a high degree of confidence.

What process did you select? _____

The next step in planning for your success is to lay out your project plan.

PROJECT PLANNING

Project planning requires a little bit of time up front, but that time is paid back many-fold during the course of the project. Although entire books are dedicated to the subject of planning, what follows should be enough to guide you through your first process improvement effort. Remember that planning is nothing more than thinking about things up-front and getting prepared. Project planning for your improvement project involves:

> *Identifying participants*
>
> *Setting specific and measurable goals*
>
> *Creating task listings and schedules*
>
> *Approval of project (if necessary)*

Identifying Participants

If the scope of the process improvement exceeds your immediate job, then other people will be needed on the project. Select participants based on their extensive knowledge of the process and/or their importance to successful implementation. Remember to include someone that can represent the customer focus. Do not exceed eight participants on the core team. Your ability to come to consensus is jeopardized when the team gets too big. You can always invite guests if you need specific expertise.

Setting Specific and Measurable Goals

Once your team has been assembled, goal setting is your next focus. Brainstorming works well to capture everyone's ideas, gripes and wishes regarding the process identified for improvement. Find the main themes that rise from your brainstorming and use these themes to provide the foundation for three or four specific and measurable goals. A common trap in goal setting is to confuse goals with solutions.

A goal states: Achieve same day delivery of all incoming mail

A solution is: Hire an additional person to assure same day delivery of mail

A key test is to ask "Will this goal allow for multiple solutions?" If the answer is "yes," then you have likely avoided the trap.

PROJECT PLANNING (continued)

Creating Task Listing and Scheduling

When all your goals are identified, it's time to begin laying out your high-level tasks and put them on a schedule. Include tasks necessary to:

- Understand and document your unimproved process

- Benchmark and baseline measurements

- Develop potential solutions

- Pilot one or two solutions

- Measure for success

- Implement the new process

Developing and tracking against a schedule is a key success factor. It's the map you need to guide you to your destination. Without it you are likely to get lost along the way.

Getting Project Approval

The team is assembled, the goals set, and a schedule in place. If you require project approval now is the perfect time to get it. The work already done will provide a sound foundation to sell your ideas and bring your project the visibility that will aid its success.

Work Your Problem!

Take a moment and review your own reactions to what you have just read.

Are you ready to put together the plan?

_____

What roadblocks are in your way?

_____

_____

How can you overcome them?

_____

_____

By this point you should have selected a process ripe for improvement. Now you should follow the steps listed in "Plan for Your Success" to get your project going!

P A R T

IV

Understanding What Needs Changing

WHERE TO BEGIN?

If you are going to give someone directions to get to your house, what is the first thing that you are going to ask them before you begin?

You are going to ask them where they are coming from. Why? Because it is a lot easier to give good directions if the directions begin at their starting point and end with their arrival at their destination. Common sense, right?

The same is true with your process improvement project. It is significantly easier to have a successful journey (process improvement project) if you begin with understanding your current location (as-is process) and then work up a set of directions (project plan) to get you to your end destination (project goals).

Begin with Your "As-Is" Process

Earlier, you learned about processes, measurements and how the customer fits into all this. Now, let's begin applying some of that knowledge. You are going to take the process you selected for improvement and carefully examine it. This examination requires an understanding of:

Inputs to Your Process

Tasks Within Your Process

Work Flow Between Tasks Within Your Process

Value Created Within Your Process

Outputs of Your Process

Measurements of Your Process

Let's break each one of these areas into the next level of detail.

WHERE TO BEGIN? (continued)

Inputs to Your Process

Inputs to your process are all the things required or consumed by your process. Typical inputs include labor, material, data and machines. Other possible inputs are time, floor space, procedures and approvals.

> **Key Idea:** The fewer and less complex your inputs, the easier it is to complete your output.

Most people are amazed at the impacts that inputs alone can have to their process.

Think of the parts, tools and skills required to assemble a clock made of non-standard parts versus a clock designed to use a few standard parts. In this example, the non-standard clock requires six different size screws and three different screwdrivers. The standard clock has three different size screws but they all work with the same screwdriver. Is that a big deal? Think about it. The hidden costs in this include:

- Ordering, receiving and stocking twice as many screw types

- Complicated instructions for assembly of twice as many screw types

- Errors in assembly

- Time lost in counting and handling multiple screw types

- Extra containers required on work bench

- Extra space required on work bench for the extra containers

- Extra movements required at work bench from container to container

- Extra movements required to pick up and put down different screwdrivers

- Extra cost of tools

Create your list of inputs required to complete your process. Be as specific as possible. Throughout all these steps, it is a good idea to check your ideas against the real-world process.

Tasks Within Your Process

Tasks are the individual steps or activities that happen within your process. Tasks can be things like assembling, filling, and completing. Tasks can also be things like counting, reviewing, telephoning, filing, and interviewing. Anything that is done within the process counts as a task. Not all tasks provide the same value to the process. The concept of "value added" will be covered in more detail shortly.

Work Flow Between Tasks Within Your Process

The steps or tasks within your process are linked by a flow. Think of the process of playing pitch and catch, which could be described as follows.

Inputs Required: Two people, two softball gloves, one ball, an open area, light

Process Steps: Person 1 puts on ballglove, Person 2 puts on ballglove

Person 1 picks up ball

Person 2 faces Person 1 and watches and waits

Person 1 throws ball to Person 2

Person 2 catches ball

Person 1 watches and waits

Person 2 throws ball to Person 1

and so on. . . .

WHERE TO BEGIN? (continued)

Flow is created when the process is put in motion. The ball sailing back and forth is process flow. The flow can be affected by things like:

- ► One good player and one not-so-good player

- ► New players who are left-handed with gloves only for right-handed players

- ► Wet playing surface

- ► Strong wind

- ► Sun in one player's eyes

The process is exactly the same in each scenario, but its flow or capacity has been affected by other factors. In other words, even though the process is exactly the same, the number of times the players throw and catch the ball in 10 minutes is less when you play with the sun in one player's eyes. The process capacity has been reduced, even though the process is exactly the same.

Situations in the workplace that could affect work flow and process capacity might be:

- ► Physical distance between operations

- ► Work being done at different rates

- ► Equipment breakdowns

- ► Material shortages

 Key Idea: A successful process improvement project considers both the process and the flow.

The ideal process flow is balanced, synchronized and continuous, which is regular, consistent and timely in the need of its inputs and in the delivery of its outputs. An example of a continuous flow process is the making of liquid soap. You keep the input vats filled, the mixers mixing and the pumps pumping, and you keep getting liquid soap as a continuous output.

Unfortunately, a balanced, synchronized, continuous flow is the most difficult type of process flow to design. Most processes are designed around a batch flow. In a batch flow, you do Task A to all the items at your workstation before you move any of the items to the next workstation. All the items wait at that next workstation to have Task B done to them. After Task B is done to all the items then they move to the next workstation and so on. Unless everything is in perfect synchronized balance, work piles up along the way. This creates shortages at some workstations and excess items at other workstations.

Let's consider an example outside of the workplace. Imagine the first time you learned how to ride a bicycle. Remember how you started to fall in one direction and you had to turn the handlebars to correct so that you didn't fall off? Those corrections were essential to staying on your bike. You had to continuously and simultaneously:

- Balance yourself and steer

- Pedal to keep going forward

- Watch where you were going

Now, imagine having three people on the bicycle all at the same time. Person 1 balances and steers. Person 2 provides the pedal power. Person 3 watches to see where you are all going. You have the combined expertise of a "Super Steerer," a "Powerful Pedaler," and a "Wonderful Watcher." Each has performed their specialty for over 10 years and is the best in their profession. Is it easier to ride a bicycle with three people or one person? The answer is one! Why is that?

One person can ride a bicycle easier because there is a continuous process flow at work. The one rider can make the corrections automatically to stay balanced and synchronized. They do not have to do something and then pass it to the next person and then wait for feedback before they do the next thing. This is another reason why a continuous process flow is more effective than a batch flow. Since you can go from step to step without stopping, you accomplish the entire process in less time. Less time usually means less cost. Would it take longer for three people riding a bicycle to get to the destination? You bet!

WHERE TO BEGIN? (continued)

A continuous, balanced, synchronized flow usually produces a higher quality product at a lower cost. In the bicycle example, how often do you think the three riders would fall off the bicycle or run over something compared to the one rider?

Let's take the bicycle example one step further. Suppose you, as an individual, rode your bike but you did all the pedaling first. Then, you would steer but not pedal or watch where you are going. Finally, after you had all the pedaling and steering done, then you would watch where you were going. Does this make sense? Then why in the workplace do we continue to insist that we do all the recording of customer complaints at one site, then move the complaints over to someone to evaluate, and then have another approve and so on? On the surface it seems to make sense. You will hear things like:

- "We have to keep the phones free to take more calls."

- "We have people who specialize in customer contact."

- "Only the supervisors can approve the resolution."

- "We have to approve the resolution before we can implement."

Take them outside and put them on a bicycle. Tell them the process goal is to ride the distance of the parking lot the fastest. First, have them ride together, on the same bicycle. Then have them ride with just one on the bicycle.

Or give them a ball and tell them that you want them to play pitch and catch. Place them five feet apart. Tell them that the process goal is to have the most pitches and catches in five minutes. For the first round, tell them that only one can throw and the other one can only catch. For the second round, tell them that they can both pitch and catch. Remember, the goal is a process output that the customer values. Any change that has a chance of doing that should be given a try.

> **Key Idea:** Get rid of the batches and the specializations and work toward continuous flow.

Note: There are times when it is good to have a specialist. If you want brain surgery, you probably want a specialist. Whether we like to admit it or not, most work is not brain surgery.

So far, we have considered:

- The inputs to your process

- The tasks within your process

- The flow of work between tasks within your process

Let's move on to discuss the concept of adding value within your process.

Value Created Within Your Process

The entire idea behind having a process is that the process creates an output that the customer values. If the customer is willing to pay for something, then they value it. If they are not willing to pay for something, then it has no value. Giving the internal or external customer something of value has to be the main reason for the process to exist. The most effective way to create a process output that the customer values is to have each task within the process add value to the next step.

Key Idea: If the customer is willing to pay for each task, the task adds value to the output. If the customer is not willing to pay, then there is no value added.

Any step or task in the process that adds value to the output is essential. These tasks usually physically change the item being worked on. There are other tasks that the customer is willing to pay for. Not all of these physically change the item, but they are also considered to be of value. Why? Because the customer is willing to pay for them. An example of a step that the customer might pay for but does not change the item is "Provide a schedule update to me on a weekly basis."

WHERE TO BEGIN? (continued)

There are two other areas that can be slightly confusing. First, how do you handle legal compliance requirements that add extra tasks to the process? Are these extra tasks adding value? The best way to evaluate whether steps driven by legal compliance requirements are value added is to ask the following questions:

► *Where does the legal compliance requirement originate?*

Track it down to the source document. Go outside your internal procedures if they reference some other external document. Get the document that starts it all!

► *What does the original legal compliance document require?*

Review the source document. It may be significantly different in its requirements when compared to your current internal procedures. Should the internal procedures be modified to reflect the true source document?

► *Can the requirements be met without these steps?*

If the source document requirement can be met without the current steps then those steps are non-value added.

The second area that is slightly confusing is the one referred to as a "necessary cost of doing business." Necessary costs of doing business are tasks that have to be done to support the overall business structure to allow the business to survive and grow. Necessary costs of doing business include tasks like:

- Renting the building

- Paying the employees

- Paying the suppliers

- Paying for insurance

These tasks, in and of themselves, do not physically add value to the product. However, if we did not perform these tasks we would not be able to even provide a product to the customer. Since these are necessary tasks to create a final product, they are considered value added.

For a task to be called value added it can either:

1. Change the product in a way that it enhances the value to the customer

2. Be an extra step, but one the customer is willing to pay for

3. Be driven by a legal compliance requirement

4. Be part of the "Necessary cost of doing business"

 Key Idea: In process improvement, the goal is to eliminate any step that is not value added.

Outputs of Your Process

The outputs of your process are things that are created by actually performing the process. Your output might be a physical item or it might be a service. The major process output should be something of value to the customer. If the process is not creating an output of value to the customer then the entire process should be questioned.

There can also be secondary outputs from the process that you might want to minimize. This could include:

- Scrap

- Noise

- Dust

- Defective finished output

WHERE TO BEGIN? (continued)

Anything that does not directly become part of the valued output to the customer should be reviewed. Look for ways to reduce or eliminate non-value added output. Look for ways to take non-value added output and turn it into something of value. Here is an example of how someone took a waste product and created a value for it. Follow the points below:

#1: In Colorado, there are a great many electrical generation facilities that use steam to run turbines that turn the electrical generators. The steam is vented outside after it has been used. It has served its purpose.

#2: Also in Colorado, there are a great many people who like fresh tomatoes during the winter. Tomatoes shipped from the warmer states are expensive and have to be picked before totally ripe to ensure they are not spoiled by the time they get to market.

#3: Greenhouses are expensive to heat during the Colorado winter.

Take these three points individually and they do not mean much. Consider them all together and you can create a new industry. In this case, some enterprising individual had the idea to build a greenhouse attached to the electrical plant and use the waste steam to heat the greenhouse during the winter to grow tomatoes for the local winter market. It all started with an observation and an idea.

Other points to consider when reviewing the outputs to the process include:

► Could you simplify or decrease the output?

► Could you eliminate this output?

► Could you add this output together with something else to create more value?

Creating and delivering a valued output is critical. In general, the more that your specific output is valued by your customer, the better. There are situations, though, where even this is not enough. As the rate of change and competition increases, these situations are becoming a way of life.

Situation 1:

Your products or services (outputs) are getting rave reviews from your customers. Your competitor unveils a product similar to yours but will deliver it in half the time at the same price.

Situation 2:

Your products or services (outputs) are getting rave reviews from your customers. Your competitor offers a product similar to yours but at 30 percent less in price.

Situation 3:

Your products or services (outputs) are getting rave reviews from your customers. Your competitor unveils a new product or service (output) that makes yours inflexible and outdated.

Situation 4:

Your products or services (outputs) are getting rave reviews from your customers. Your competitor hits you with the triple whammy. He offers a product superior to yours, delivered in half the time at 30 percent less in price.

Key Idea: Having customers raving about your product or service today, does not guarantee that you will have customers raving about your product or service tomorrow.

WHERE TO BEGIN? (continued)

You may be reading this thinking:

> ► "But I just work in one of the lower level processes, what can I do?"

> ► "My output is not the finished product."

> ► "Management has the responsibility for this."

There are things that you can do. You can bet that the competitor mentioned in Situation 4 has everyone at the company working towards the same goal. Any company that can deliver a superior product, in half the time, at 30 percent less price has to count on everyone, in every process, to contribute.

You can start to contribute by just thinking about what processes you are involved in. Think about them in the context of what we have discussed so far:

- The inputs to your process

- The tasks within your process

- The flow of work between tasks within your process

- The outputs to your process

There still is one part that must be included. You need to be willing to measure your process.

Measurements of Your Process

Earlier, we discussed the overall subject of measurement. Keeping these ideas in mind, you need to get specific about the measurements of your process. At this point, you are just collecting data on the existing processes as they are currently functioning.

You are probably in one of three situations. You are either in:

Situation 1:

> No one has done anything with measures. There is little, if any, historical data or current data.

Situation 2:

> There are some measures in place. There is some historical data and/or current data.

Situation 3:

> There are good measures in place. The measures are focused on what is important to the customer. They may be measuring even more. There is some historical data and current data to work with.

If you find yourself in Situation 1, then you really have to start from scratch. Start with only three measures in the beginning. Let your customer tell you what the most important things are, and then measure those. If possible, try to measure things that repeat within at least a week, preferably shorter. The reason for this is so that you can check progress without having to wait for six months.

If you find yourself in Situation 2, then you have to decide if the current measures are of value and generate good data. At this point you should gather any existing information from the current measures already put in place. You should also spend some time learning what the measures are actually measuring and how well they work. Spend some time and talk with the people that create the data. Again, ask the customer what they think the most important things are. If the current measures are not measuring what the customer thinks is important, then implement at least one new measure that is important to the customer. Monitor all the measures.

If you are lucky enough to find yourself in Situation 3, then all you have to do is gather up the historical and current data and monitor it.

WHERE TO BEGIN? (continued)

Measurement of the process is the final building block necessary to understand your current "As-Is" process. The process that you selected to examine can now be broken into the following to describe its "As-Is" condition:

- The inputs to your process

- The tasks within your process

- The flow of work between tasks within your process

- The value that is created within your process

- The outputs of your process

- The measurements of your process

This is quite a list of items to consider as you are examining your current process. Fortunately, there is a tool to capture this information. It is called a process map.

CREATE YOUR OWN PROCESS MAP

A process map is a handy tool to gain a better understanding of your process. It is especially useful when you have a complicated process to examine. A process map begins as a picture of all the things that happen within your process. In some cases, it is easier to start at a top level and then work your way down to the lower levels of detail. If you are already very familiar with your process, you may want to start at the lower level. As a suggestion, there should be no more than 10 tasks at any one level.

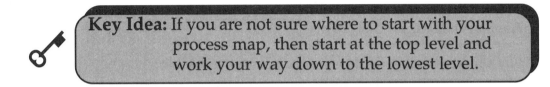

Key Idea: If you are not sure where to start with your process map, then start at the top level and work your way down to the lowest level.

A process map for a company that builds decks on the back of homes may look something like this:

A Process Map Example for "Decks 'R Us":

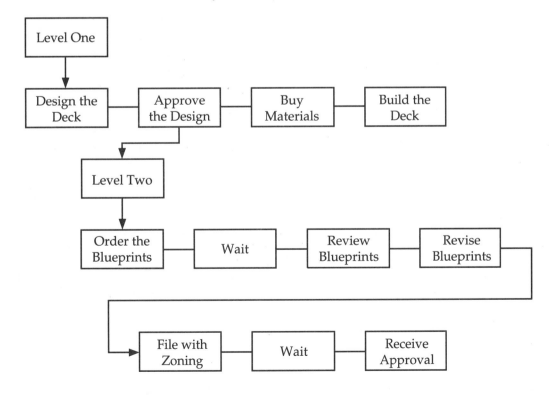

A process map is beneficial when you want to see the flow of your process.

CREATE YOUR OWN PROCESS MAP (continued)

A Process List Example for "Decks 'R Us":

You can also choose to create a process list instead of or in addition to a process map. A process list for the same flow looks like this:

Tasks for Level One	Time
Design the Deck	5 Days
Approve the Design	30 Days
Buy Materials	1 Day
Build the Deck	5 Days

Total: 41 Days

Tasks for Level Two	Time
Order the Blueprints	.1 Day
Wait	5 Days
Review Blueprints	.4 Day
Revise Blueprints	.5 Day
File with Zoning	.5 Day
Wait	23 Days
Receive Approval	.5 Day

Total: 30 Days

Process lists work best when you are trying to total times or other resource requirements.

PROCESS MAP AND
PROCESS LIST GUIDELINES

There are several guidelines to follow when creating a process map or list. They are:

► Follow one item through the entire process. Follow that one item in what- ever state it normally goes through the process. If it goes through as a batch, then follow it as a batch. If it goes through as an individual item, then follow it as an individual item.

► Identify what really happens to the item, not what is supposed to happen to the item. Many times what actually occurs is significantly different from what the work instructions say.

► List every single step that happens to the item including errors, inspections, exceptions, wait time, moves and anything else that happens. These steps that are not part of the usual process can be gold mines of savings.

► In addition to listing every single step, capture how long each one of those steps takes.

Note: Assigning times to every single step in the process can be a daunting task. Do not make this into a project killer. Measurements do not have to be to the "third decimal place." Make time assignments to steps quick and easy by using any of the following suggestions:

• Simple, direct observation and record the results.

• Existing measurements, if the data is credible.

• Operator estimates, usually in conjunction with one other method.

• Temporary measurement systems to collect results for a short period.

• Existing records to back into a measurement.

When creating any part of the process map or list for the process you selected, work with the "hands-on" people. Hands-on people are the ones that are actually doing the work. They know what they have to do to get an item to the next step of the process.

Key Idea: Create your process map or list with hands-on people.

PROCESS MAP AND PROCESS LIST GUIDELINES (continued)

Once you have created your process map or list, then the next step is to check the map or list against the real process. There are several ways to check your map or list:

- Walk through the process and compare each step to the map or list.

- Ask the hands-on people to OK your map or list.

- Add up the time required by your map or list and compare it to the real process.

You are now ready for the final step that will allow you to gain some significant insight into your "As-Is" process. You are now ready to identify the parts of your process that add value versus the ones that do not add value. This is easier said than done.

Determine if Each Step Adds Value

Your task now is to take your process map or list for each step in the process and classify it as either value added, non-value added or "not sure yet." Ask yourself the following question for each input and step within the process:

What would happen to the end output that the customer values, if I eliminated this input or step?

If the answer is *nothing,* then the input or step adds no value and should be marked as non-value added. If the answer to the question is *something,* then the input or step adds value (at least for now) and should be marked as value added. If you run into some steps that do not have a clear answer, don't get hung up. Just mark them as "not sure yet" and come back to them later.

As a suggestion, mark the corners of the boxes for the non-value added tasks. The extra marking makes the non-value added tasks stand out. These are the ones to concentrate on.

When you get done with this particular activity, your map or list should look something like this:

Value-Added Process Map

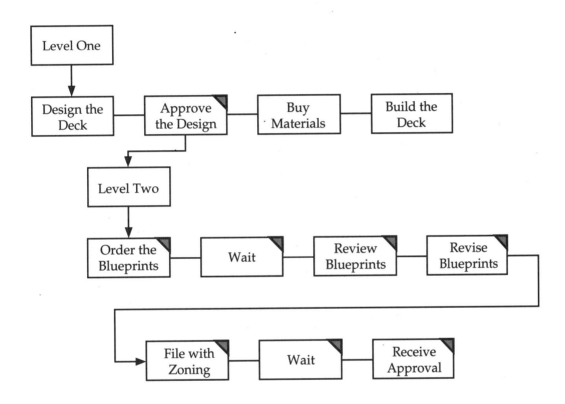

The reason why "Approve the Design" is marked as non-value added is because you checked with the local city government and found out that you did not have to submit deck designs for approval as long as you were a licensed building contractor. You already had your license, so all you had to do was eliminate this step. Your business is booming!

PROCESS MAP AND PROCESS LIST GUIDELINES (continued)

Value Added Process List

In a value added process list, the times are actually listed in their correct column. This makes it very clear what adds value and what does not.

Tasks for Level One	Value Added	Non Value
Design the Deck	5 Days	
Approve the Design		30 Days
Buy Materials	1 Day	
Build the Deck	5 Days	

Tasks for Level Two	Value Added	Non Value
Order the Blueprints		.1 Day
Wait		5 Days
Review Blueprints		.4 Day
Revise Blueprints		.5 Day
File with Zoning		.5 Day
Wait		23 Days
Receive Approval		.5 Day

Congratulations!

You now know how to create a process map where:

- Each input and step is listed

- Each input and step is timed

- Each input and step is identified as either value added or non-value added

- The map is agreed to by hands-on people

If you do these four things for your process, you will be in an enviable position. You will have achieved a thorough understanding of your "As-Is" process. You will be in a position to make significant improvements to your process and increase the value of the output to your customer.

Take Advantage of Work Already Done!

Many times different people within an area will attempt to get something going and then it dies. Before you charge out to create your process map, ask what has been done in the past. It is certainly OK to use what other people have already created as a starting point. There is no need here to reinvent the wheel. You do want to take the time to verify that whatever was done before is still current. If the last process flow was done three years ago and everything has changed since then, do not spend too much time with it. On the other hand, you can learn from past projects. If you can, get them for your review.

PROCESS MAP AND PROCESS LIST GUIDELINES (continued)

What to Expect at This Phase

Doing the "As-Is" is hard work. It requires attention to detail. It requires the willingness to write things down. It requires a willingness to ask questions and not pretend like you know it all. Does this sound like fun to you? Not me!

You can expect to get lots of pressure, from yourself and others, to just skip all this and start changing the process. Resist this temptation!

There are traps here. If you start changing steps in your process without a thorough understanding of the impacts, you run the real chance of impacting the customer. You also run the risk of starting something that may cost more to finish than you estimated. There is also the real chance that your changes may be the best for you, but you have hurt other processes that are depending upon you.

If you skip the "As-Is" phase, the biggest value that you will miss is your increased understanding of how the process really works. You will never know what powerful changes you could have made because you grabbed onto the first one that caught your attention.

Since you don't want to fall into any of those traps, resist the temptation and do the steps listed here in Part IV. There is one last trap to mention. It is a very easy trap to fall into.

BEWARE OF BECOMING STUCK IN THE "AS-IS"

There are tons of details to work in creating the "As-Is." Just as it is a bad idea to skip creating your "As-Is" model, it also is a bad idea to get stuck in perpetual "As-Is-ing," getting so caught up in the details that you forget your end goal. Your end goal is increased customer value. If you cannot get past the "As-Is" phase, you cannot accomplish your goal. Give yourself a time limit for the "As-Is" phase and work towards it. Remember that you do not have to have all the information to move forward. There is a balance.

Work Your Problem!

You have already identified the process that you want to improve. Now it is time to create the "As-Is" model for the process. Create a value added process map and process list for your process. Include times for each step in the process. Be sure to consider the following when creating your "As-Is" model:

► The inputs to your process

► The tasks within your process

► The flow of work between tasks within your process

► The value that is created within your process

► The outputs of your process

► The measurements of your process

P A R T

V

Getting Where You Want to Be

IDENTIFY THOSE PESKY PROBLEM AREAS

We cannot become what we need to be by remaining what we are.

—Max De Pree

The "As-Is-ing" is complete and now it's time for the exciting part. Your next steps are:

- ► Identify the ways to eliminate as many non-value added steps as possible.

- ► Analyze the process for additional areas for improvement.

- ► Sketch out the plan and implement the changes to create a new process.

Eliminate Non-Value Added Steps

First, begin by asking one very important question. "Is this process that I am evaluating even necessary?" Time and money can be spent improving a process that you don't really even need. Some of your processes may have come into being based on a requirement that no longer even exists. Eliminating processes is the greatest time and money saver of all!

If you have decided that your process is necessary, then review your non-value added steps in the process. It would be nice if all you had to do was just stop doing the non-value added steps. Unfortunately, if you eliminate the non-value added steps without understanding why they were put in place, you could soon find yourself with a process that does not work at all. Take the time to understand the cause of the non-value added steps. Understanding will make it easier for you to eliminate the non-value added steps and design a process that produces a valued output.

IDENTIFY THOSE PESKY PROBLEM AREAS (continued)

There are a few main reasons why non-value added tasks normally creep into existing processes. After all, when the process is first thought up, no one sits around and says "Let's create a process that wastes a lot of time and money." When you focus on your non-value added tasks, you are probably looking at a task that was put in place to minimize the impact of one or more of the following issues:

Backlogs of Work

Errors and Quality Issues

Hand-offs Between People or Organizations

Physical Movement of People or Work

Changeover Times of Equipment or People

Dealing with the Unpredictable

If you can figure out how to eliminate or minimize these items then you have a very good chance at eliminating the non-value added steps that have crept into your process. Let's take a look at each one of these issues in more detail.

Backlogs of Work

Those backlogs of work stacking up everywhere mean long cycle times and poor work flow. Whenever you have a backlog, you normally have non-value added tasks in your process flow that might include:

- Wait time or items in backlog

- Counting of items in backlog

- Report status of items in backlog

- Storing of items in backlog

- Expediting of some items in backlog

To find out how deep of a hole you are in, you can create a measurement indicator of Days of Backlog. You can identify this measure for the entire process or just one step in the process. To figure your days of backlog use the following formula:

$$\text{Days of Backlog} = \frac{\text{Items in Backlog}}{\text{Daily Item Output}}$$

Your goal is to eliminate the backlog. If you eliminate the backlog, then you eliminate the non-value added steps associated with the backlog. Here is an example:

The Backlog

It took the purchasing department an average of 22 days to place a purchase order. This was hard to understand because it only took a buyer an average of four hours to actually process the paperwork. The formula above explained the problem. The daily output of the department was 20 purchase orders. The number of requests waiting in piles was 440. That meant each request sat around 22 days, working its way from the bottom of the stack to the top, before a buyer would be able to spend the four hours necessary to process the order.

Use the backlog measurement as an indicator that change is necessary. Your goal is to get as close as possible to just-in-time processing. In the example above, that would mean that you should redesign your process to make the time from "receipt of request" to "actual purchase order" as close to four hours as possible. By doing this you could eliminate the non-value added tasks tied to the caretaking of the backlog. How do you eliminate the backlog? The first step is to look at putting all the personnel resources that handled the backlog (the counters, expediters, and statusers) and put them to work performing the value added tasks. Other methods for coming up with solutions will be discussed at the end of this section.

IDENTIFY THOSE PESKY PROBLEM AREAS (continued)

Errors and Quality Issues

Error checking, scrap, rework, inspection and control points all indicate a process that has quality problems. These problems waste time and lead to non-value added activities. Non-value added activities can be eliminated if we eliminate the source problem.

You will want to focus on two measures to better understand your quality problems:

▶ The number of errors within a task

▶ The number of items reworked to correct problems

Within each category there may be many causes. You need to collect information at the most basic level so you can discover the underlying problems that cause these errors. Fortunately, there are usually only one or two problems that create the majority of the errors. The trick is to identify the underlying problem. By asking the "five Whys," we can help uncover the root problem. Here is a good example:

PROBLEM: The bread is inconsistent in its browning. The loaves exit the ovens burned 17 percent of the time.

WHY? The temperature is set too high.

WHY? The bakers don't reset the temperature early enough to allow it to cool down.

WHY? The bakers don't always know what will be baked next until it's being loaded in the ovens.

WHY? There isn't a consistent pattern to the way the baking is done when special orders are part of the shift.

WHY? There is not a unique schedule or plan in place for shifts which contain special orders.

From the above example you can see the underlying cause of the burned bread was a lack of scheduling for exceptions. If the bakery had not dug deeply for the root, it would be easy to assume that the bakers were just sloppy in their attention to oven temperature. If sloppiness was the root cause, a solution may have been to post a sign or a reminder to the employees about the importance of temperature. Now that the real root cause is understood, the bakery can do some planning in their bakery schedule to take into account oven temperature needs for special orders. Sometimes you need to ask a lot of questions to get to the underlying cause!

Key Idea: Ask the five Whys to get to the root cause.

Hand-offs Between People or Organizations

Hand-offs occur when work passes from one person to another or from one organization to another. It could be from the stock clerk to the shipping clerk or from the purchasing organization to the accounts payable organization. Hand-offs add a great deal of complexity and usually a large amount of non-value added steps to your process. Go to your process flow and identify every time there is a hand-off.

It is important to pay attention to hand-offs because there is usually at least one wait with every hand-off in your process. These wait periods cause the work to move in batches which interrupt your continuous, balanced, synchronized flow. Also, depending upon the trust level between organizations (or individuals) there may be counts, sign-offs and status reports required before a hand-off can even occur.

After you have identified all the hand-offs in your process, you can create another measurement indicator of the health of your process. Since processes vary in complexity and length, the total number of hand-offs is not necessarily significant. You want to look at the number of hand-offs per value added task. Strive for a ratio of less than one. You want to minimize the amount of hand-offs in your process.

$$\text{Hand-off Ratio} = \frac{\text{Hand-offs}}{\text{Value Added Tasks}}$$

IDENTIFY THOSE PESKY PROBLEM AREAS (continued)

If your hand-off ratio is greater than one, take a look at where you can begin to eliminate hand-offs by:

- Cross training individuals to do more than one step in the process

- Combining organizations

- Transferring the total process into one organization

Physical Movement of People or Work

Every time there is a hand-off, work moves, people move, or both move. Work or people may also move without a hand-off. If you do a task and then carry the work to another location to perform another task, the work has moved.

For example, you have a job as a cook in a restaurant. The food is stored in the freezer at one end of the kitchen, it is prepared at a station in the center of the room and cooked at the opposite end. Many moves are involved in retrieving, preparing and cooking the food.

Movement is a non-value added activity. Like hand-offs, movements usually result in at least one wait. That wait is another non-value added activity. (They sure add up fast!) Other hidden non-value added items could include:

- ▶ Equipment to move the work (forklifts, trucks or carts)

- ▶ Space to be able to move the work through

- ▶ Wasted time in movement (different from wait time)

- ▶ A person being away from their desk or workstation

Usually it is easier to see the amount of movement tied to your process if you draw it out on a piece of paper. You will be amazed at the miles that your work or you travel.

Key Idea: Plot your movements visually by drawing lines on a diagram of the work area.

You probably have figured out by now that you can create yet another indicator of the health of your process. You can measure the number of movements in a process compared to the number of value added tasks.

$$\text{Movement Ratio } = \frac{\text{Movements}}{\text{Value Added Steps}}$$

If your process is movement heavy, then look for places to reduce the number of moves.

Changeover Times of Equipment or People

Usually when people think of changeovers they think of machine set-up time. While that is an example of one kind of changeover, there are many others that may be less obvious. Stopping in the middle of a copying job to add paper to the machine, holding for the telephone order taker to get his terminal up and running to take your order, waiting to charge gas at the service station while the computer system does an every-50-transaction charge summary—all of these are examples of changeovers within a process.

Not all changeovers result in substantial time loss, but they all interrupt the flow of work. All of them are non-value added activities! The longer the changeover time, the greater the impact to the work flow. When long changeovers are part of a process, you will find a degree of inflexibility in operations and larger backlogs of work in process. This is due to a desire for larger batch sizes so that there will be longer times between changeovers. (A vicious cycle!)

To reduce changeover time consider some of the following:

- ► Have tools and supplies ready before beginning the job.

- ► Eliminate as many control points, inspection checks and approvals as possible.

- ► Make sure the person doing the changeover has detailed instructions which describe easy-to-follow, sequential steps.

 Key Idea: Reduce changeovers to improve flow.

IDENTIFY THOSE PESKY PROBLEM AREAS (continued)

Dealing with the Unpredictable

In a perfect world, work would come into a department in a steady, even stream with no peaks and valleys. Every task in the process would take exactly the same amount of time to complete and the work flow would be continuous. Unfortunately, few live in this perfect world. The number of inputs to the process may vary from day to day and from week to week. Some tasks may take longer to complete causing work flow problems. The people completing these longer tasks may feel pressure to hurry which can result in errors.

Usually the way we cope with this unpredictability is to create non-value added tasks that buffer the process from the unpredictability. The "buffer" approach usually includes non-value added things like:

- Inventories
- Underutilized employees
- Work-In-Process backlogs
- Underutilized equipment

A better way to address unpredictability is to either:

a. Tackle the underlying causes of unpredictability and reduce unpredictability.

or

b. Understand the cycles of unpredictability and plan for them.

To tackle the underlying causes of unpredictability and reduce it you may need to:

▶ Spend some time with your supplier of inputs and negotiate new arrangements for delivery of inputs or change suppliers.

▶ Review your maintenance schedule on your equipment and perform preventive maintenance to prevent unexpected breakdowns.

▶ Log your incoming calls for a period of time to get an understanding of peak calling periods.

To understand the cycles of unpredictability and plan for them, you may wish to consider:

- Cross-training so that multiple people can do whatever is required.

- Arranging to have a few people on-call to respond if needed.

- Subcontracting work if needed.

Remember, buffering the unpredictabilities with extra inventories, people and equipment increases non-value added costs. Other people have figured out ways to address unpredictabilities without these additional costs. You can too.

IDENTIFY THOSE PESKY PROBLEM AREAS
(continued)

So Many Issues and So Little Time

Note: All of the underlying causes and issues are just as applicable to an office or service environment as a manufacturing environment. They may just not be quite as obvious.

As you can see, there are many different issues to consider. Sometimes the underlying causes are difficult to discover. Sometimes even once you understand the underlying cause, you may not know exactly what to do about it. Here are some thoughts.

First, *you* are the expert when it comes to your process. Don't lose sight of your experience and common sense. Analysis tools are just that, tools. It is the mind behind them and the hand that uses them that gives them power! In most cases, the people performing the process already know what to do once they have had some basic process improvement training.

Second, several tools have already been discussed that you can use to help solve potential roadblocks. You can use any of the following tools and techniques to help you if you are stuck:

- Brainstorming

- Ask why and keep asking until you reach the underlying cause

- Trial and error

- Experiments and tests

Key Idea: Don't make this too hard, use your experience and common sense as the starting point.

COME UP WITH EFFECTIVE OPTIONS

As your analysis progresses, options begin to surface. You see where non-value added steps can be eliminated, cross-training can occur, organizational boundaries redrawn and work flows simplified. One word of caution here: There is a tendency to want to immediately leap to one favorite or obvious solution. Resist that tendency and challenge yourself to develop multiple options to the problem.

This is the time to maintain an open mind and stretch past the boundaries that were acceptable in the past. To stretch your thinking set a goal for the number of different options you want to identify. Outrageous thinking can sometimes lead to very creative options!

After your initial list of potential options is developed, begin reviewing the feasibility of each option. You may need to check with a supplier, run the option past a design engineer or investigate legal issues. You should be ready now to start narrowing in on the preferred solutions and designing the improved process.

SELECT THE RIGHT SOLUTION

Once you have your options defined, it helps if you have clear criteria in place so you can rate the options. If you were selecting a solution to reduce an increasing backlog of mail in the mailroom you might include cost, ease of implementation, customer response and probability of solving problem as your criteria for selection. Once you know how you will measure the choices, the comparison becomes much easier! A ratings chart can make the choices visible as in the example below.

Rate 1–5
1 = Not Preferred
5 = Most Preferred

	Cost	Ease of Implementing	Customer Response	Probability of Solving Problem	Totals
Add Staff	2	4	5	4	15
Out Source	3	1	4	4	12
Departments Pick-up	5	2	1	3	11

When the ratings are totaled, adding staff is the preferred option based on the criteria.

 Key Idea: The more objective your evaluation, the more accepted your solution.

A ratings table is just one way to identify a solution from the list of choices. Depending upon your project, you may find that all you need to do is to spend some time discussing the options with someone else before deciding on the solution to implement. Take advantage of all the experience, knowledge and resources that are available to you. Remember, do not turn this portion of the project into a never ending task. You can always adopt a solution and then adapt it as you gain experience with it. Continue to move forward and adjust as you proceed.

 Key Idea: You can always adopt a solution and then adapt it as you gain experience with it.

Whatever you do, realize that you have to change the way things are currently.

PLAN YOUR IMPLEMENTATION

You may feel you are home free at this point but for many people implementing can be the most difficult step. Implementing change requires planning, persistence, planning, good execution skills and more planning. A great tool during this step is a detailed milestone chart which displays the key steps of the implementation. This chart should have dates associated with each milestone.

Implementation Plan	Week Ending				
	5/6	5/13	5/20	5/27	6/3
Plan gets approved	◆				
Combine pilot assembly and test workstations into one		◆			
Rewrite new assembly and test instructions		◆			
Complete new doorway from assembly to shipping			◆		
Train operators			◆		
Begin using new process				◆	
Present first pass findings					◆
etc.					

PLAN YOUR IMPLEMENTATION (continued)

In addition to your milestone chart you will want to create a task listing which provides further definition. The task listing identifies the detailed tasks as well as the person responsible for completing each task.

Task	Responsible	Due Date	Completion Date
1. Plan approval	Sue	5/4	
2. Incorporate changes	Bob	5/5	
3. Set up operator meeting	Sue	5/6	
4. Conduct meeting	Andy	5/10	

Communication is critical during implementation to help keep those affected by the changes tied into the process. The rubber meets the road at this point so preparation is your key to success. Provide leadership to assure follow-through on all assignments and meet regularly with those involved to offer support, encouragement and focus. If you discover that things aren't unfolding as you had planned or that things surface that you forgot to address, don't abandon your plan, *change it!*

Follow Through after Implementation

Now is your opportunity to re-measure using the analysis tools that helped you to identify the changes. Your measurements should show improvements that can be quantified. If you don't see improvements initially, you may want to wait for the process to settle down for a short time and measure again. If you still aren't seeing the improvements you had hoped for, go back to and re-evaluate your root cause. It may take some practice to really get to the root of the problem.

Provide a lot of acknowledgment during this step, to those who helped to make it happen as well as to yourself. A pat on the back is due! Celebrate your success and take the time to broadcast your accomplishments. One person's or group's success is a great motivator to others.

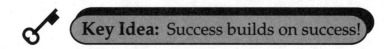 **Key Idea:** Success builds on success!

Begin Again

Process improvement requires a continual focus on the customer. Since the expectations of the customer do not stay static, your improvement process must continue. You will not want to focus immediately on the process that you just reviewed, but select another and keep on improving for success. Your business depends on it!

What to Expect at this Phase

Just as in the other phases, there are some common reactions to expect at this point. Feeling overwhelmed was mentioned before but it is worth repeating. Many people are uncomfortable with analysis because they think it is difficult and complex. Keep it simple and beware of analysis paralysis. You can get stuck in the details of the decision process and never come out the other side.

If you do the evaluation work you can expect the 80/20 rule to apply. Twenty percent of your changes will drive eighty percent of the improvements. You can get a lot of benefit with a small amount of the **right** change!

With any change you can expect resistance. You are now at the point of putting something new in place. You will experience less resistance if participation has been a focus. The more a person is a part of the solution, the less resistance you will see!

PLAN YOUR IMPLEMENTATION (continued)

Work Your Problem!

Pick a process in your area that you have previously identified. Using the information you have been given so far in this book, work through the problem as follows. (Work this exercise through on another sheet(s) of paper.)

1. Define your goal, i.e., what is your key area chosen for improvement.

2. Gather data using the "As-Is" view of your existing process. Be sure to identify non-value added steps and cycle time for all steps.

3. Identify the underlying issues, including an underlying cause analysis.

4. Develop multiple options or solutions. Once the list is developed, investigate the feasibility of each option.

5. Select a solution. Make sure that you have rated each option using clear criteria. (Resist the temptation to make this step more complex than it needs to be.)

6. Implement your solution. Create your plan and task list and stick to it.

7. Review (remeasure) the outcome of your changes. If you don't see improvements by now, go back and re-evaluate your underlying causes. Don't give up now!

8. Acknowledge everyone involved and ensure that everyone gets proper credit. Think up a fun way to celebrate your success.

9. Begin again. Remember, process improvement requires continual focus on the customer. Keep looking for ways to improve.

Getting Changes to Stick

IF NOTHING HAS CHANGED, YOU MISSED THE MARK!

The entire reason you invest time and energy in a process project is to change things for the better. If you cannot get your changes implemented, then have you accomplished your goal? If you get your changes implemented and three months later everything is back the way it was before, then have you really changed anything?

Too many projects end up with these two problems:

- Great analysis, no implementation. Project dies.

- Great analysis, OK implementation, no follow-through. Project dies.

Many companies and individuals invest in the up-front training for process improvement. Some companies and individuals will actually follow-up and try a project. A smaller number actually get to the project implementation stage. An even smaller number will implement, but let the project die a slow death. Unfortunately, too few actually implement, follow-through and reap the rewards. So close and yet so far.

The major reason that these projects die is because companies and individuals forget the end goal. They lose their focus and momentum. They start thinking that the end goal is the number of people trained in process improvement. That's where the trouble starts. Everyone can see through this. "Oh no," they think, "another 'all talk and no action' program." It is easy for people to make that type of program a low priority. Remember that the end goal is increased customer value! Increased customer value had better not be a low priority if you want to stay in business. Process improvement is just a means to that end. The companies and individuals that recognize the goal are much more likely to keep their focus and make change stick.

> **Key Idea:** The end goal is *increased customer value.* Process improvement is just a means to that end.

> **Key Idea:** *Increased customer value* has to be the *goal* on a daily basis!

Increased customer value will result if you get your project implemented and keep it implemented. It is OK to stack the deck in your favor to make this happen!

WORK THE "FOUR P'S"

The best way to stack the deck in your favor is to work the "four P's" which are:

People

Plan

Process

Priority

Let's walk through the "four P's" one by one.

(**People**)

By definition, people are going to be involved in whatever reengineering and process improvement project that you do. At the least, this will include you and your customer(s). At the most, this might include your customer(s), your peers, your supervisor, your subordinates (if you are a supervisor) and yourself. People power is what makes process improvement work. Getting the players to commit their heart and brains is a critical factor to your success. How do you do this?

You get people power to work for you when people own the project. If they feel that process improvement is something that is being "done to them" then they will likely react in a negative way. People who feel included and are part of the project will be more likely to support the project. People who feel that the project is the "flavor of the month" will just ignore it.

You unleash people power by creating individual ownership. You create individual ownership by:

- Honestly explaining what you are trying to do and why.

- Asking for help. Let each person know you need their individual expertise.

- Asking them to give it a trial period. Nothing has to be etched in concrete.

- Letting everyone involved see a part of themselves in the project.

- Following up. If you start something, finish it!

These guidelines are true whether the people involved work for you or you work for them. Get people invested in the project. Make them want to see the project succeed. Get excited! Get them excited!

⬭ Plan

Trying to create and implement a successful process improvement project without a plan is like going on vacation to a strange place with no map. As long as you do not care where you end up or when you get there, it works fine.

Planning is normally one of those things that everyone knows that they should do, but never get around to putting down on paper. Visions of two-feet-long schedules and volumes of detailed documents make us hesitate to even begin the planning process. It is so much more fun to just start doing rather than planning.

Actually, planning is not quite as tough as most people think. Keep in mind that for your plan to be effective it must be a living, working document. Try to think of your plan as:

- A personal tool.

- Short and covering the major phases of the project.

- Easily understood.

- Updated and changed as necessary.

- Having an end date and a follow up date.

WORK THE "FOUR P'S" (continued)

Process

A considerable portion of this book has been devoted to process. A process view is critical to getting change to stick! Take a minute and review the following:

What is the glue that ties all our tasks together?

> ***Process!***

What is the framework that we use to understand what tasks we do now?

> ***Process!***

What allows us to tie together our inputs and outputs?

> ***Process!***

What allows us the thread to cross functional organizational boundaries?

> ***Process!***

What gives us the structure to identify and eliminate most non-value added tasks?

> ***Process!***

What makes it easy to measure our progress?

> ***Process!***

What allows us to focus on what is done versus who is doing it?

> ***Process!***

What is the first word in process improvement?

> ***Process!***

(Priority)

If you expect process improvement to produce any meaningful results then "doing things differently" has to be a priority. Process improvement creates major threats to the status quo. The status quo has lots of energy behind it. It is easy to stick with the status quo.

STATUS QUO	DIFFERENT VIEW
Process improvement is just the latest buzz word. Just wait it out and things will get back to normal.	In fact, process improvement is just using your common sense to better satisfy your customer. Make it a priority to use common sense to better satisfy your customer.
You say that you support process improvement. You study a few processes and then make virtually no change. You claim process improvement doesn't really make that much difference.	Make it a priority to take your idea for improvement all the way to implementation and then, after implementation, make sure that you give it another three months to see what really happens. If it works, that's great. If it doesn't work, then at least you have gone the full distance and can go back to the way it was before the change. Please note that if you stick with the change for a full three months you might run into a funny phenomenon. By then, the change will be the status quo and no one will want to change it back.
You are too busy doing your current job to take on the extra job of process improvement. Your priority is putting out the fires.	If you are too busy to spend any time looking for ways to change and improve your current job, then you probably need process improvement more than anyone. Your priority has to be fire prevention not fire fighting.

WORK THE "FOUR P'S" (continued)

How do you make process improvement a priority?

Set aside some time and just do it! This does not mean that you have to spend forty hours a week working process improvement. To start, take one hour a week and try some of the things suggested in this book. You can start with something easy. You usually eat sometime during the day, so how about trying the following:

► Take a customer (internal or external) to lunch and ask "What are some things that we could do differently that would make what we do for you more valuable?"

► Take an inspector to lunch and ask "What could we do differently to reduce rejections?"

► Take your boss to lunch and ask "What are the major problems within our department?" "What can I do to help?"

► Take a peer to lunch and ask "What is the major problem that you have in getting your job done?" "Would you like to help me do something about it?"

We all have exactly the same amount of time available to us. The only way you can change for the better is to take the time to do it. Take the time by making "change for the better" a priority. After you make a change for the better, keep focused on that change until at least three months after implementation.

Key Idea: Focus on the four P's of **People, Plan, Process** and **Priority** to make your change for the better stick!

A PATH TO AVOID

There is another way to make process improvement a priority. It certainly is not the recommended way, but many take this path. Some take this path knowingly, but most take this path because they don't know another way. They wait and do nothing. Finally, when the wolf is at the door, fear becomes the major motivator. You lose a major account or two. You start hearing talks of layoffs or of a merger. Change suddenly becomes a major priority.

To put this into a more personal example, it is like waiting until your first heart attack before you begin your exercise program. Unfortunately, nature's wake-up call comes to companies as well as individuals.

When you think about it, process improvement can be compared to an exercise and diet regimen. If you exercise and watch what you eat, there is still no guarantee that you won't have a heart attack. Still, research shows that the odds in your favor of not having, as well as surviving, a heart attack are significantly improved. The same is true with process improvement. If you work process improvement on a regular basis, the odds that you will come out on top are significantly improved. The good news is that process improvement projects can be more fun than dieting while you ride your stationary bicycle.

A Case in Point

The following real-life case is an example of how easy it can be to gain the benefits of process improvement and increase the value that you give your customer:

The Overnight Shipping Consolidation

BACKGROUND: The company has offices in three major locations dispersed across the United States. The company depends heavily upon overnight shipping services to get original documents distributed among the three major locations in a timely manner. The company is spending $80,000 a year on overnight delivery services with an outside overnight delivery business. The internal company department that is responsible for the shipping function is committed to making continuous improvements and supports all department personnel who want to make a change for the better.

"As-Is" PROCESS: The company shipping clerk is the focal point for the collection of the individual overnight delivery packets. Each person who needs something delivered overnight to another location gets an empty overnight shipping envelope from the secretary, addresses it, places the document inside, seals it and takes the packet to the shipping clerk down on the dock. The shipping clerk logs each packet into the overnight shipping companies computer terminal and then takes all the packets up to the lobby at the end of the day for pick-up. The company is charged $8.95 for each individual packet shipped.

A PATH TO AVOID (continued)

ANALYSIS: The company shipping clerk decided to look for a way to reduce overnight shipping costs. After making a few phone calls, the clerk discovered that the overnight shipping company charged $8.95 to ship a box that could hold at least 20 of the individual packets. The clerk counted the number of individual packets for a one month period and kept track of the end destinations. The clerk discussed the situation with his supervisors to let them know what he was doing.

IMPLEMENTATION: The clerk attended a meeting of the company secretaries and asked for their help in changing the current process. The clerk presented the data and suggested an alternative to the current process. The alternative was to place a pre-addressed box for each of the three major "ship to" locations by the front door. Anyone who needed overnight delivery would still fill out their individual envelope just as they have been doing. Instead of bringing it to the shipping clerk, they would place it in the proper box on their way out of the building at the end of the day. The shipping clerk would close all the boxes at the end of the day and give it to the overnight shipping company courier for shipment. If there was an overnight delivery to some location other than the three major "ship to" locations, then their packet would be placed in the fourth box labeled "Other." The shipping clerk would then separately handle all the "others." Some minor changes were made and the change implemented.

RESULTS: After the change, the clerk counted the number of individual packets that went into each box for a one-month period. That count was used to estimate the savings. This simple change provided the following benefits:

- ✔ The company's overnight shipping costs went from $80,000 a year to $30,000 a year. This represents a true savings of 63 percent.
- ✔ The clerk did not have to spend the time to log-in each individual packet.
- ✔ It was more convenient for the people to drop off the packets at the end of each day while going out the front door instead of going down to the dock.
- ✔ The cost to implement was less than $1000.
- ✔ The clerk was so excited by the change and the results that he has gone on to several other projects. All his projects have had similar results.

The point is that you can change things for the better at any scale, at any level within a company. If you are an individual clerk, you can make a difference. If you are a team leader or the company president, you can make a difference. You do not necessarily have to invest in new million dollar computer systems to increase the value that you give your customer. You do not have to use every tool in this book to make a difference. But you have to get started. You have to stick with your project all the way past implementation if you want to see results!

IMPLEMENTATION: WHAT TO EXPECT AT THIS PHASE

Right about implementation time, you may begin to run out of steam. You have stuck with it and now it feels like it is time for a rest. Don't stop! Every day that you delay implementation:

- The risk is increased that your changes will never live to see the light of day.

- The risk is increased that someone will come up with another excuse to maintain the status quo.

- The risk is increased that a critical member of your team will get reassigned to some other task or part of the company.

Right about implementation time:

- ► You may begin to get stiff resistance from people who might be affected by the change and were not involved in the project. They now understand that the proposed change might actually occur. They are going to offer advice—after the fact. The best response to them at this point is: "Let's try it for awhile (three months) and if it doesn't work then we can either modify it or change it back." This is a very reasonable offer that is difficult to fight. Again, most people, after they do something for three months will not want to change it back. It has become the status quo.

- ► You may have second thoughts about the project. You may become concerned that all this is not going to work. This is a natural feeling. Don't worry. If you have worked the four P's then you have stacked the cards in your favor. Also, keep in mind that if something doesn't work the way you anticipated, you can always change it.

IMPLEMENTATION: WHAT TO EXPECT AT THIS PHASE (continued)

Right after implementation:

▶ Expect problems. Things will not go exactly as you thought. You forgot one detail and that caused a back-up in the packaging area. You eliminated the final inspection process, but you forgot that the final inspector put the company label on the product. Five hundred units were shipped without the company label. Although you cannot foresee what the individual problems will be, expect them. Plan to have the time available to work out these problems. This is not the right time to take a two week vacation. Schedule some time to talk with the people most affected by the implementation. Get out and stay in touch with what is happening.

▶ Expect the doomsayers to pick up on the problems and use them as reasons why things should never change. Ignore them. Focus on making the change work.

A couple of months into the implementation, you can expect a shift. The doomsayers get quiet and become suddenly interested in something else. The measures are showing that the change was for the better. Nothing takes the wind out of doomsayers' sails better than facts and data. The people who supported the project become more vocal and excited. Nothing creates excitement like success! At this point morale has improved and people feel like they really made a difference. You are also feeling pretty good about yourself. Now is a good time to celebrate the success. Results have been achieved.

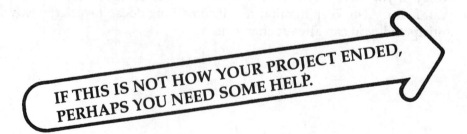
IF THIS IS NOT HOW YOUR PROJECT ENDED, PERHAPS YOU NEED SOME HELP.

HELP!

Asking for help is sometimes a difficult thing to do. No one likes to admit that they can't do it all. A good thing to remember is that when you ask for advice, you still can decide if you want to follow it or not. Once you decide that you want some assistance, then it helps if you know what type of help you want.

Two Different Types of Help

There are two different types of help that you might find valuable. You might need either "content" help or "process" help.

Content help is based upon a specialized understanding of your particular business. You are asking for content help if you need help in determining what machine is most cost-effective in meeting the new part tolerances that your customer now requires. If you are in the muffler design business and you want your mufflers to last 20 years, then you might call in a metals expert to give you advice about new metals available to extend muffler design life.

Process help is based upon a specialized understanding of how process improvement projects work regardless of the particular business. You are asking for process help if you need help with your first attempts at making change for the better a way of life. If you have tried to change for the better and keep falling short, then you call a process specialist.

If you don't know what kind of help you need or are not even sure you need help, your first call is to get process help.

HELP! (continued)

Where to Go for Help

Some larger companies have internal resources that are available. They may have both content and process specialists ready to assist with your process improvement projects. Check to see what resources your company has available.

The second place to go for help is outside the company. Going outside the company for help has some major benefits and drawbacks.

Benefits of using specialized help outside of the company include providing:

- A perspective free from your company culture and history

- A broader perspective through working with many companies

- A more specialized expertise by developing one talent

- Assistance that can be let go at any time so you only pay for what you want

- Tools so you do not have to reinvent the wheel and you can get moving faster

Drawbacks of using specialized help from outside the company:

- Internal people can feel threatened

- More expensive when compared hour for hour to internal personnel

You have to be the one to make the decision. There is no doubt that there are firms that will sell you multi-million dollar answers to your thousand dollar problems. There is also no doubt that you could save time and get moving faster down the path of "making a change for the better" if you had some outside assistance. Most people understand the value of content help. Process help is not quite as well understood. There are different strategies you might want to consider for effectively using process help. Use a process specialist to:

- ▶ Provide an initial assessment and recommendations. Once you have the initial assessment and recommendation, you are free to do what you think best.

- ▶ Train all employees in an area targeted for change. By transferring basic process improvement skills to people within the company, you only have to pay for their training, they already work for the company.

► Start a "Train the Trainer" program. This is where the process specialist trains a few internal company personnel on process improvement techniques and then the internal company personnel take it from there.

► Help a team that is stuck.

► Be involved at the startup of an improvement team looking at a critical area of the company.

► Help the hands-on personnel set up their own measures.

There are many other possibilities. There are many paths that can lead to a successful process improvement project. Remember that the goal is continuously increasing customer value.

HOW TO MAKE THIS A CONTINUAL PROCESS

Different cultures around the world emphasize different things. Different companies around the world emphasize different things. The one thing that is becoming a requirement for cultures and companies alike, all across the planet, is change.

> **Key Idea:** To merely survive, you must accept change. To thrive, you must actively embrace change.

Whether we like it or not, the rate of change continues to increase. Not only is there an increased rate of change, but there are also more variables to consider. You have to consider foreign economies. You have to consider legislative developments. You have to consider cultural differences. And the list goes on and on.

Depending upon your perspective, an increased rate of change and an increased amount of variables to consider can be viewed as a wonderful thing. Anything can happen! If you are Number 3 in your industry, you have a very real chance of becoming Number 1. With nothing more than a personal computer and a fax machine, you can nibble away at the industry Goliath who has been in business for 20 years.

Some people refer to the time we are living in as chaotic. Some people want to offer ways to avoid the chaos. They believe that the model of centralized hierarchical control is not only still possible but preferred in times of chaos. Unfortunately, all of the benefits of having centralized hierarchical control are more than negated by several small details.

► **More Decisions Are Required!** The increased rate of change makes more and more decisions necessary.

► **Faster Decisions Are Required!** The increased rate of change means decisions have to happen faster and faster to be timely and meaningful.

► **Variables Are More Complex!** The increased amount of variables to consider (local and non-local, internal and external, national and international) makes it difficult to have any preset plans in place.

► **Customers Are More Demanding!** Customers are expecting more customized goods and services. One size does not fit all.

- ► **Customers Are Even More Demanding!** Customers' quality and value expectations are increasing daily.

- ► **Employees Have More Ownership and Stake in the Outcome!** To get meaningful change to stick we have to have involvement and ownership by the people making the change.

- ► **Middle Management Is on the Ropes!** Middle- and lower-level management is in shock with all the changes happening. They are searching out new roles and trying to avoid losing their jobs until they figure out what to do.

- ► **Every Day It All Is Happening Faster and Faster!** All these changes are continuously happening faster and faster.

So What Is the Logical Response?

To Management: Get the employees involved. Get the employees and the managers together. Give them responsibility and accountability. Give them the opportunity to use their head and heart in making the business successful. If you feel that they are not ready yet, then train and educate them. Give them overall goals or, better yet, let them set their own. Then get out of their way. Whether at the lowest department level or the top executive level, the prescription is the same.

To Everyone: Wherever you are in your company, if you want to be part of a growing, thriving organization then you must make it a priority to increase your customer's value on a continuous basis. The way that you do that is to get yourself, and as many people in your company as you can, the basic skills necessary to make continuous change for the better a way of life.

READERS SPEAK UP

Please write us and let us know about how this book works for you and the experiences you have with your project. Any suggestions for improvement from you, the customer, are always welcome!

We would like you to let us know how your project went. We would especially like to know:

1. What did you find really useful in this book?

    _____

    _____

    _____

2. What would you suggest we change and why?

    _____

    _____

    _____

3. What project did you pick and what happened?

    _____

    _____

    _____

☐ I would like more information about Delta Solutions, Inc. workshops for Process Improvement, Team Building, Facilitation and Customer Service.

Name (optional): _____

Organization: _____

Address: _____

City, State, Zip: _____

Telephone/FAX: _____

Please mail or FAX to: Delta Solutions, Inc.
                           9457 So. University Blvd., Suite 328
                           Highlands Ranch, CO 80126
                           (303) 683-9760   FAX (303) 683-9759

Can we use your example: ☐ Yes   ☐ No

NOTES

NOTES

NOTES

NOTES

NOW AVAILABLE FROM
CRISP PUBLICATIONS

Books • Videos • CD Roms • Computer-Based Training Products

If you enjoyed this book, we have great news for you. There are over 200 books available in the *50-Minute*™ Series. To request a free full-line catalog, contact your local distributor or Crisp Publications, Inc., 1200 Hamilton Court, Menlo Park, CA 94025. Our toll-free number is 800-442-7477.

Subject Areas Include:

Management

Human Resources

Communication Skills

Personal Development

Marketing/Sales

Organizational Development

Customer Service/Quality

Computer Skills

Small Business and Entrepreneurship

Adult Literacy and Learning

Life Planning and Retirement

CRISP WORLDWIDE DISTRIBUTION

English language books are distributed worldwide. Major international distributors include:

ASIA/PACIFIC

Australia/New Zealand: In Learning, PO Box 1051 Springwood QLD, Brisbane, Australia 4127
Telephone: 7-3841-1061, Facsimile: 7-3841-1580   ATTN: Messrs. Gordon

Singapore: Graham Brash (Pvt) Ltd. 32, Gul Drive, Singapore 2262
Telephone: 65-861-1336, Facsimile: 65-861-4815   ATTN: Mr. Campbell

CANADA

Reid Publishing, Ltd., Box 69559-109 Thomas Street, Oakville, Ontario Canada L6J 7R4.
Telephone: (905) 842-4428, Facsimile: (905) 842-9327   ATTN: Mr. Reid

Trade Book Stores: Raincoast Books, 8680 Cambie Street, Vancouver, British Columbia, Canada V6P 6M9.
Telephone: (604) 323–7100, Facsimile: 604-323-2600   ATTN: Ms. Laidley

EUROPEAN UNION

England: Flex Training, Ltd. 9-15 Hitchin Street, Baldock, Hertfordshire, SG7 6A, England
Telephone: 1-462-896000, Facsimile: 1-462-892417   ATTN: Mr. Willetts

INDIA

Multi-Media HRD, Pvt., Ltd., National House, Tulloch Road, Appolo Bunder, Bombay, India 400-039
Telephone: 91-22-204-2281, Facsimile: 91-22-283-6478   ATTN: Messrs. Aggarwal

MIDDLE EAST

United Arab Emirates: Al-Mutanabbi Bookshop, PO Box 71946, Abu Dhabi
Telephone: 971-2-321-519, Facsimile: 971-2-317-706   ATTN: Mr. Salabbai

SOUTH AMERICA

Mexico: Grupo Editorial Iberoamerica, Serapio Rendon #125, Col. San Rafael, 06470 Mexico, D.F.
Telephone: 525-705-0585, Facsimile: 525-535-2009   ATTN: Señor Grepe

SOUTH AFRICA

Alternative Books, Unit A3 Sanlam Micro Industrial Park, Hammer Avenue STRYDOM Park, Randburg, 2194 South Africa
Telephone: 2711 792 7730, Facsimile: 2711 792 7787   ATTN: Mr. de Haas